MUSINGS: BLACK WOMAN WHITE WORLD

Helen Akangbe

This memoir is dedicated to My 3 Ns Nathaniel, Nathania, and Nathaniella: mummy loves you forever. I have no favorite I promise.

WELCOME TO HELEN.

"If we were meant to stay in one place, we'd have roots instead of feet "Rachel Wolchin

Hello dear reader, how are you doing today?

I like to welcome you to my world, birthed from a beautiful black mind, inspired by a richly proud African heritage, and nurtured by an amazing western culture and lifestyle. Every day, all over the world, life sometimes necessitates the need for a person to leave their home, to seek residence in a new place, country, or even continent. This change consists of the many required adaptive measures, from learning a new language, trying a new cuisine, or even living amongst an unknown race, culture, or lifestyle, all of which can be daunting or even scary. You might be a black person living in the western world, or a Caucasian, Asian or Arab, living in Africa or on some new continent wherever that maybe, but know that your struggles are not peculiar, for you are not alone.

This memoir is inspired by my feelings, thoughts, and experiences after leaving Nigeria in West Africa as a young adult, to join my mum and siblings in the United Kingdom. My journey in the United kingdom started with living with my parents as a single black girl, to getting married to a "what would I do without you" husband David who sweeps me off my feet or drives me raving mad (my version of the truth) depending on the day! and becoming mother to three, amazingly beautiful, unique and mind-blowing (I mean this literally!) children. I remember my first concern on arriving to the united kingdom, was how my new British neighbors would view me: would they regard me as an equal person, or as the underprivileged, black girl from the stereotypical charity videos depicting African children as sickly and starving? Thankfully, I was fortunate to find myself amongst people who were quick to regard me as an equal, and treated my family similarly, helping me to evolve into a confident, astute woman who understands the importance of staying true to oneself in every situation.

Over the years, I have been able to collect many memories along the way, the good, bad, and ugly lot of them, and I apologise now for my impending ramblings as your read on. I have met many people, tried and loved some new cuisine, embraced a new culture, and thoughtfully adapted my lifestyle to compliment my new country. I have dabbled into many ventures like social work, the civil service, online business, and nursing, whilst an intrinsic dislike of voluntary driving scared me from applying to be a bus driver, probably a blessing in disguise for the poor commuters who might have been sentenced to my endless chatting and off-key singing. In the likely occurrence that you wonder how my lovely, madcap mind works whilst reading the book, just smile, laugh, cry or grimace and embark on this womanly and insanely wondrous journey with me. Now is the time to attempt that wry smile.... and turn the next page. Welcome to Helen's world.

MUSINGS EPISODE 1: MY WAY OR INTUITIVE INTELLIGENCE?

"You have your way. I have my way. The right and only way does not exist." **Friedrich Nietzsche.**

How do I begin to introduce myself to you? Okay, kindly allow me let you into my consciousness, my grey matter aspect case in point my brain and will-power. Do I like to have my way or do I have a very good mind? I do not know exactly which to be honest, but I would define myself as an objective, compassionately intelligent person with a knack for solving problems or finding solutions that actually work. I am an extroverted, friendly, hopeless romantic with a crying guarantee when watching emotional movies. I am very emotional with a deep sensitiveness to my loved ones, unfortunately making me susceptible to hurt from them. I frequently question myself if a giving person an express power to hurt me is a weakness, as I find myself easily becoming emotionally invested in family and friends, a gesture mostly appreciated, but sometimes declined by the recipient kicking me out of their lives directly or indirectly. Alas! When this occurs, I just withdraw, become indifferent after the hurt and anger phase, and watch whoever they are from a distance.

I believe my analytic and realistic approach to life frequently earns me the tag of a problem solver, adviser, or counselor. However, on some occasions and with some particular persons I have been unfortunately deemed as pedantic, opinionated, or adamant on having my way. I have even been told I have an either my way or the highway attitude to situations, but I beg to defer. Nonetheless, I must confess that I usually feel an avalanche of frustration, when I see a sure cracker way of approaching a situation or fixing something, and the other person does not, and I try to persuade them to see things from my perspective or just give up. I am unapologetically unable to go halfway with people or pretend to save face, well my face is my biggest traitor it gives me away all the time: you know when I am happy, sad, frustrated, angry or indifferent as soon as I step in a room. I am objective, and do honestly consider myself to be very intuitive, hence my gripe when sometimes others disagree with me: for instance when my sister Mary, brother Ayo, or sister in law Tomi argue with me, all I can think is how dare they! Laugh. However, in other circumstances when I argue with my husband or my mum and I find myself losing to them, either due to ingrained respect or frustration, I just cry.

I love to research and find out information on different topics ranging from education, careers, business, money, love, relationships, people to holidays and travel you name it, you say something I find out information about it. That is how I live, acquiring knowledge. Sadly, I have stopped reading a much books as I used to, but I still try a lot to monetize my time or just put value to it, so my social media interactions is minimal less than 10 hours a week, as honestly if I cannot employ an avenue to better myself then it is a waste of valuable time. Being able to acquire verified information through diverse on and off line mediums such as the bible, mentors, books, journals, biographies, true-life stories, interviews, blogs, and forums, has made me a well-informed, problem solver. But I still do ponder if I just love having my way all the time, or that I am very intuitive and intelligent so mostly right anyway, or a mixture of both? I will leave that for you to decide ...wry smile please.

MUSINGS EPISODE 2: IT IS
OR NOT MY HAIR

*"Life is short, you might as well live it with really great hair "***Anonymous.**

I am a proud Black British woman, and my most defining characteristic, asides from my largely light brown skin colour, is my hive of semi long black hair. Growing up in Africa I have loved long hair, my mum Elizabeth and elder sister Florence had very long hair, whilst I had a good amount just enough for people to comment 'is that your hair'? A comment guaranteed to make me smile. On moving to United Kingdom, I continued in the "my hair is the best" mood, until the year 2009, when I shockingly discovered that in the United Kingdom and really in the western world, my hair was not regarded as the 'best' type of hair texture, and that hairdressers would charge the moon, or sometimes I could swear they were aiming for the stars, to make my hair. For reasons I am yet to understand, I found myself bemoaning why I did not at least have the hair if not the skin colour of other races, yes, I admit I do envy the other races for a moment or two, before common sense intervenes to remind me that black is beautiful! Funny you might say, maybe not, but I guess it is only human to desire what others have even for a fleeting moment.

Anyway, so began the race to pretend to not have my kind of hair, which was not so difficult to achieve as all around me most black women I knew that is family, friends, and colleagues jumped on the 'it is my hair it is not my hair' bandwagon. The market became flooded with all sorts of cheap to very expensive hair products ranging from £40 to an excess of £1000, targeted to the African consumer, all of which were mostly owned by non-black companies or manufacturers, which makes me wonder why we consumers have failed to invest in an industry where we are the main income generators, food for thought. Moving on to the undeniable feat of choosing a the supposedly perfect hair, firstly, you get to choose one of many names like Brazilian, Mongolian, Peruvian, Remy, then the eye watering specifications of weft, gravity (thickness), treatment, dye, colour, bleach, virgin, or non-virgin wow! Who knew hair has virginity status? Then finally the application type: wig or none wig, frontal, side, free, two, or three parts, my goodness! black women are very intelligent with all the information we have to digest and apply, and we are just at hair!

Initially, I defied the urge to jump on the bandwagon, and stuck with perming or braiding my hair, but could not persevere when all my home girls looked way different from me at parties and in pictures, and yours truly became the plain Jane relegated to the 18th century. Thus, when my sister Mary offered me a Brazilian hair product for my birthday, I said yes, as I honestly could not afford it. Since joining the trendy hair craze, I have discovered two funny aspects to wearing fake hair, both pertaining to my Caucasian neighbors, friends, or colleagues. Firstly, I hear comments and questions like "did you change your hair? /is that your hair? / your hair is so beautiful how did you make it like that? Or I get a plainly confused look from those who find it hard to understand why today I am a straight, bob, blond and tomorrow a curly brunette with long stresses, considering Caucasian women only wear wigs, or for stage plays, theme parties, and not for everyday life, except due to unfortunate hair loss as a side effect of chemotherapy. Secondly, the funniest thing is whenever I wear a wig for occasions, as soon as I enter my car or walk through my front door, my first action is to frantically yank the wig off, scratch my pained, tired, hot scalp, breathe a sigh of relief, and get some fresh air in! Never ceases to make me laugh, and I never fail to question why I do this to myself.

Good news! 2018 brought along the natural hair trend. Starting from the west to Africa, most sisters ditched their expensive wigs and weaves, cut their hair and started growing it again from scratch, but along came an endless list of natural hair products which were much more complicated, and expensive than the products used by those who perm their hair. I always say to black women, to convince me you have natural hair, you have to be like my mum Elizabeth, grow your hair using only two products a good conditioner and coconut oil and nothing else! Disclaimer! Please do not get me wrong, I respect every woman's decision on hair choices, so long as we are sure that we have not been shamed into thinking our hair is not beautiful. I will not shout cultural appropriation when I see a non-black woman braid or cornrow her hair, as we spend all that money on hair that is not like ours, do you get me? The question is whose fault is it? Do we blame society for passively or actively suggesting to us through movies, social media, advertisements and posters that beauty is defined only by possessing pale skin and long silky hair, or we who are gullible enough to believe our beautiful glowing dark skin and thick kinky hair is not beauty personified? I choose to be re-sponsible for my life's choices, how I define myself and measure beauty, for at the end of it all, when I take off the wig or weave, wash my black, kinky, full hair, style or just tie it in a bun, is when I feel most beautiful, free and most importantly real.

MUSINGS EPISODE 3: I AM NOT YOUR SISTER

"Discrimination does not make anyone great, instead, it makes us weak" **Anonymous.**

I will tread very carefully on this episode of musings as I understand that racism and discrimination is a sensitive subject, albeit one that has been around from time immemorial has been a subject of real pain, shame, and even denial for some. Unfortunately, some people have abused the concept, using racism as a weapon to hurt others, or to have their way in life, throwing up the race card for different reasons in order to achieve a goal. In 2016, I took the plunge and decided to commence my degree in nursing, after dabbling in the many career paths mentioned in the foreword, and I am to introduce you to the happiest children's' nurse in the world! In Nigeria where I grew up nurses followed a hierarchy system, respect across bandings is taken seriously, thereby sensitizing me for life. Interestingly, my most poignant memory of racism occurred within this fine profession.

In the United Kingdom, most nurses and indeed other members of the multidisciplinary team tend to be decent, inclusive, and informed people who view everyone as equal. During my nursing training in the southeast England, I was required to work alongside registered nurses, hence my automatic inclination (or you could say my African sense of respect for elders kicked in) to address this about to retire nursing sister, whom I was assigned to work with one fine morning as sister (her name). I approached her and said good morning sister (her name) with a smile, but was unprepared for her next move when gently grabbed my arm, put it next to hers, looked me in the eye, and asked, "How can I be your sister"? I was so shocked, my mind went blank and for the life of me could not utter more than a short "really"? That action and sentence stayed with me throughout the day, and it boggled my mind that someone so educated and selfless, to be a paediatric nurse for over 20 years, could be so short sighted and shallow, and poorly informed about inclusion and tolerance, that she would determine sisterhood by only skin colour. Considering that the racism culture is sometimes a cluster action, I was not surprised that in my remaining time on that particular ward, one of her nursing colleagues once referred to me as her happy slave because I was so efficient! I was determined not to feel victimized, or discriminated against, but concluded their actions was not a slight towards who I was, but was a loss to them, nonetheless, I made it a point to report her to my university head of nursing studies, who promptly took it up with the matron and hospital, as said nurse had coincidentally had prior incidences of similar nature.

Of course, we British are quick to judge the Americans as being blatantly racist; well to be honest one can easily justify this assumption, considering some of the racial occurrences that occur on the other side of the pond are not even fathomable here. Sadly, the increasing spate of tragic shootings, even now public tree hangings of black people by vigilante neighbors, the police and unconfirmed persons alike, makes the United kingdom a heaven for a black woman like me, as I would be in hell if I thought my 13 year old Nathan could be shot by a racist policeman for walking home from school for any random reason he can conjure. That said, in as much as the British people are inclusive, non-bias and respectful of everyone, with an absent feeling of inequality and opportunity, there is this unspoken, underlay of racism so subtle that you run a risk of not finding it even when it stares you in the face. For example some BAME (black and ethnic minority) friends and colleagues are so scared to eat their favorite cultural dish at work, for fear of it being deemed as stinky or unappetizing, but every food smells and your perspective of it being a good or bad smell, depends on your knowledge of the said food, as they said beauty lies in the eye of the beholder, so let us be more tolerant of others' cuisines I would say.

Regardless of this awareness, I must confess it is very easy for me to forget I am black in my day-to-day life, I consider myself British, and that is enough 99% of the time. I strongly believe my life will not be different if I was a white woman living in the united kingdom, so I always tell my kids, extended family, black friends, associates especially the young ones, to do their best to utilize every opportunity as one is mostly to blame for ones' failures. My take is that, we must be tolerant of everyone we come across in our lives journey, respect their space, colour, faith, values, and belief. Life is uniform, we matter equally, and no one race or color is more beautiful, intelligent, special, than the other for every opinion is based on the holder's perspective.

MUSINGS EPISODE 4: IDENTITY CLASH OR BI-IDENTITY

"Be who you are and say what you feel, because those who mind don't matter, and those who matter don't mind." **Dr. Seuss.**

I unavoidably got an identity clash on moving to Britain as a young adult. At home with my parents, I am 90% African and 10% British, and once outside the percentages swap rather effortlessly, and without a sense of guilt or feeling of fraud. What makes me 90% African at home is the language, food, culture and relationships. For starters, I get to speak Yoruba a southern Nigerian dialect freely with my parents and siblings. Our diet, is largely African rice stapes like Jollof and fried rice, pounded yam, plantain, stew, okra, yam, beans and other African delicacies with a dash of western foods like cereal, toast, pancakes, salads, jackets and roast dinners. Home culture includes television, religion, and day-to-day family life, our television is multi-faceted, we enjoy western television mostly channels from the popular Sky TV, but we also use television as a connective medium to get updates about the Nigerian economy, news, easing our nostalgia by watching African moves, and listening to African music. For relationships, we maintain a large extended family unit of which I am fortunate to have grandparents, uncles, aunties, cousins and in laws in the united kingdom, and for family friends, we keep the rules simple: respect everyone, and every older woman or man is addressed as uncle and aunty no questions asked, oh what the love!

As a married adult the statistics remain largely unchanged in my own home, albeit we watch way less Nigerian television now, as I have since moved from Indian, to Turkish cinemas and oh what the joy! Turkish movies and especially their series is the bomb! I even follow pages and groups on Facebook, and I get to watch both cinemas on Netflix and YouTube. The other difference is I only get to speak Yoruba with my husband, as we have not gotten round to teaching our children aged 13,11 and 7 Yoruba yet. However, it is hilarious watching them attempt some words, as they do know phrases and words and are keen to learn, just that time and energy are not available to teach them. A part of me hurts that they might never experience the joy of speaking that wonderful language, but I must confess my children are more British than African, and happily so. We still have a large extended family now that my siblings are all married with kids, and regarding family friends: my children understand that every older African woman or man are addressed as sir and ma, and other adults are generally addressed by their titles, with my husband and I painstakingly defining who exactly is uncle and aunty to the kids, to prevent a continuation of the confusion. The other aspect of our Africanism is that we are Christians, and it is the norm in our home to participate in daily evening bible study, praise, and prayer, although we give it a twist to make it informative fun for the children, and some of our bible and life application debates will crack you up.

Like I earlier implied, outside of my home I become 90% British, my accent unconsciously changes slightly so everyone understands, I speak in a lower pitch as there is a running joke that African kids grow up hearing their parents shouting, and learn to talk on loud pitch, which people unfortunately feel is brash, intimidating or aggressive but it is not the intention, we just have natural microphones. I enjoy my universal meals; I love English, Chinese, and Turkish cuisine, like filled jacket potato, special friend rice, or Turkish bread or pizza, not forgetting bread and butter pudding or baklava. I am keen to discuss all the sky drama, latest BBC series, trending Netflix movies, I debate about British politics, education, business, economy, the royal family, the National HealthService (NHS), the great British bake off, B-list celebrities, and the weather. I am tolerant of all or no religion, and find it easy to start a conversation with colleagues, friends, and neighbors.

Overall, I am happy both at home and when out and about, and I have decided rather than continue to feel like my life is a tunnel of identity clashes, I will embrace and enjoy both my identities, and happily classify myself as Bi-identity, free of confusion, guilt, or worry. There is nothing wrong with being a slightly different you as occasion warrants, and being multifaceted is how you adapt and integrate effectively in today's ever-changing world.

MUSINGS EPISODE 5: JOLLOF RICE

"Pull up a chair. Take a taste. Come join us. Life is so endlessly delicious." **Ruth Reichl.**

I f I omit to muse about this well-loved African food, my musings are not complete and you will not completely know me. My number one African one-pot rice and tomato staple is jollof, fondly referred to jollof rice paying obeisance to the main ingredient. This meal has been cooked in various African countries with more than one of them laying claim to being the originator, you should hear Djimon Hounsou and D'banj argue comically about the country originator of Jollof on instagram. Point to note that rice is a simple carbohydrate, with a high glycemic index, hence my slight aversion for it in large quantities due to diabetes type 2, blood glucose spiking and weight gain, although research has argued rice on its own does not cause weight gain.

Jollof rice is made by boiling rice and adding a blended mixture of tomato, chili (or not), sweet pepper and onions, with some oil, salt and bouillon cubes to taste or adding boiled and drained rice to the fried mixture and steaming until dry. You can add anything to garnish and the list is endless from vegetables, seafood, meat, and poultry or enjoy it plain. I recently discovered post a scary diabetes diagnosis that long grain rice could be alternated with low Glycemic index grain bulgur wheat and cooked in the same manner, hereby getting the same dish with a gentler effect on blood glucose, good for pre and confirmed type 2 diabetics. The good news therefore is that jollof can be modified by using grated cauliflower or bulgur with the same cooking ingredients albeit the rice.

In my crazy mind, I honestly feel we Africans have committed a big disservice by not making jollof an English staple like the Indian curry and Chinese fried rice. It is a calamity that Jollof is not a global meal today, as it has the uncharted appeal to cut across language, race, and regions. I guess it is achievable, any ideas how we could go about this? I cook a lot with mostly good to very good feedback from those who consume my cooking, however, I wish I had the time, knowledge or enthusiasm to start a cooking show, or vlog on YouTube, Facebook or Instagram showcasing African foods like Jollof rice. I wish I could introduce the joys of this food to an international audience, in a bid to make it global whilst making tons of money on the side, but alas! That is not my forte, but maybe you can globalize my Jollof? There is some food for thought.

MUSINGS EPISODE 6: HOLIDAYS

"Take vacations, go as many places as you can, you can always make money, you can't always make memories" **Anonymous.**

I am a person of very few indulgences. Unlike most women my age, I rarely feel the need to visit the spa, fix nail extensions, or have perfectly groomed hair. I do not wear designer labels, I have an overflowing closet full of largely unused high-street label shoes, bags and dresses with a sprinkle of high end labels: not Prada I mean Jasper Conran. I love fine dining and the hubby and kids are hooked as well. I also enjoy a good movie, with Cineworld cinemas being my go to leisure hub, and proof is my fourteen years Cineworld unlimited membership, which allows me watch movies everyday, every week for a flat monthly fee. Being a nurse means, I hardly wear home clothes to work, and with my social calendar only filled with random restaurant and cinema visits with the hubby, I find no major use for fashion. We are halfway through the year now, and I am yet to attend one party, and no it is not because of the coronavirus pandemic, my calendar has been pretty much the same for the last six years or so.

Now to my one true love, my main indulgence, my sweet sin...

drum rolls...Holidays! Yes, a holiday is described as an absolute period of leisure and recreation, or travel specifically spent away from your home. The typical black family do not go on holidays away from home when off work and school, and you must understand that I took my first holiday as an adult, although we usually flew to my dad's work station during holidays in Nigeria, and that is the point you see. Holiday is the absence of the doorbell ringing, bills, letters, visitors, house or any kind of chores, regular routine and most especially compulsory work. I put my hand up and say work for me is not fun, if I win the lottery today, I will retire and work on a voluntary basis I promise. I plan my holidays way ahead and tend to have weekend getaways with the hubby thanks to my resident sister in love Tomi, for whom I will be crying for a completely different reason when she gets married soon, and I am not ashamed to tell her that. The hubby and I mostly have British city breaks like Birmingham, although we have ventured abroad to Amsterdam, Ireland and to Lisbon, which was an unforgettable experience when we missed our Lisbon flight due to an accident occurring about ten minutes from the airport, resulting in us literally watching our plane leave, although we got to fly out the next day without penalties.

We take holidays with our kids at the beginning of their ten-week long summer break in early july, saving loads on holiday costs as we travel before the general summer holiday breaks:a fantastic positive about private schools. Our favourite European destination is Spain,specifically Magic Natura water and animal park in Alicante Benidorm, an absolute ultra-all-inclusive haven, and holiday home for the last seven years, where we usually spend a week or so, considering the British are holday lovers and often holiday for aneye watering fourteen days or more! If only yours truly could afford that. In the last week of August, we drive down to our British all-time favourite staycation, Butlins Bognor Regis in Sussex for a five night stay . I understand Butlins is a love it or hate it destination, but I swear the hotels and half board premium dinning option beats any holiday abroad, plus you are assured of getting an English sausage and Heinz baked beans for breakfast, international standard pantomime and circus show, a fair ground, indoor waterpark, activities and many more all included on site, so what's not to love? For the odd Easter holiday, we visit any of the Canary Islands all-inclusive resorts in Tenerife with the lovely mountains or Lanzarote where you can see live volcanic mountains and eat lava-cooked chicken. I only ever stay at al inclusive resorts when travelling with the kids, why you wonder? I have once lived the horror of having kids on a holiday, and trying to find food to satisfy three age groups of children, and two adults with very different taste buds, and it was pure torture for the lack of a better adjective.

From my ramblings above, you must have deduced that although I love luxury holidays, I am also an unapologetic foodie, albeit with a very non-adventurous taste bud that prompted me to visit at least three Turkish restaurants in London, before venturing to Antalya in Turkey for a holiday in December 2019, my latest holiday discovery. For December weather, Antalya was sunny enough to warm us, as most 5-star all-inclusive having heated indoors and outdoor pools, with only a winter concept and minimal activities and entertainment. The resort we stayed at, the Rixos Premium Belek was paradise, felt like Dubai on half price with twice the level of luxury. The resort passed my holiday tick list, a true 5-star rating that included but was not limited to pre-arrival customer service, food quality, ambience, water activity, on resort or nearby beach, kids entertainment, various a la carte, shisha bar, 9 bars, kids club, teen club, sports, gym, indoor and outdoor pool, hamman and spa, a nearby sister hotel land of legends that has free entry for guests, the list is endless.

Food for thought: holidays do not have to break the bank or be 5 stars: it is going somewhere, anywhere you can afford comfortably and have some time to rewind, rejuvenate, relax, reflect, plan, or bond with family and loved ones if you have one. On holidays, we like to dress up on a night or two, for a la carte fine dining on resort, because for some reason our holidays combine as birthday getaways as well. The only challenge I have with holidays is that we are a family of five, and finding resorts with sleep 5 rooms is a real struggle, thus restricting our options of hotels and resorts options. Thankfully, all the resorts we have been to have rooms and suites that can sleep five, which is a real blessing. My holiday advice is to book flights, ferry or trains at least five months ahead, drive, for accommodation, check trip advisor reviews and use the questions options, compare accommodation prices on comparison sites like booking.com, compare prices with direct booking, as most are pay on arrival so you can change your mind up to a day before arrival without paying penalties. It might look like I am lucky enough to afford holidays, but the truth is something has got to give, so one can cut back on the expensive designer jewelry, outfit, weekly manicures or that expensive hair piece, some other personal luxuries and spending, because frankly if I can, then anyone can.

MUSINGS EPISODE 7:
CORONAVIRUS SARS 2

"Perfect health, like perfect beauty, is a rare thing; and so, it seems, is a perfect disease". **Peter Latham**

Here I find myself writing this chapter at the end of July 2020, on a topic that never existed when I started writing this memoir. Thinking back to January this year, the several tense warnings from the World health Organisation (WHO), scientists, and experts about the impending arrival of the coronavirus SARS2 virus (COVID-19) into the United Kingdom, and the very ignorantly unwise decision to disregard these warnings, the first cases of COVID-19 in the United Kingdom were confirmed on January 29th in the city of York. The initial reaction was of denial about the authenticity, infection rate and virility of the virus, closely followed by astounding shock about its' brutality, with the unseen virus killing hundreds of people per day worldwide, cumulating in a never before seen country lockdown. The country went into lockdown mode, and COVID-19 guidance from the government came into effect in relation to every aspect of our lives. Firstly, we all suddenly got cut off from extended family, friends, and work colleagues with places of worship, businesses, and schools shutting, except essential food shops. Initially there was a mad rush for food, drinks, household items, and maybe you heard of it or participated in the toilet roll madness! People queued for hours and fought over loo rolls, eggs, flour and hand sanitizer, clearing aisles and making it next to impossible for others to buy. It honestly felt like Armageddon, but we as a family tried our utmost best to remain calm and unaffected from the chaos, by stocking up on African food supplies, which weirdly became slightly more expensive but was still available.

My kids' schools shut just before the Easter holidays, I continued working, until my husband who had begun home working started having a new persistent fever and mild cough, earning me two weeks of self-isolation at home, and only allowed back to work after a negative swab test, in accordance with the COVID-19 guidance. We had to cancel our Easter holidays to Istanbul and spent the entire lockdown period literally watching television, having family time, taking walks, cooking and baking new recipes. We started going for family walks with the kids in the evenings, wearing facemasks and gloves and maintaining the required 2-meter spacing between others and us. Getting off the curb when coming across another person caught on, and a cough in public space was enough to make even the cats run for shelter. Easter was horrible, no church, no family lunch, and heartbreakingly my mum could not see or hug anyone of us because we had to stop meeting her physically, trying to shield her, even though she is very healthy. Nonetheless, on a slightly humorous note, bras, corsets, girdles, makeup, grooming disappeared and visits for manicures, massages, hairdressing, gyms, and to restaurants all stopped. Life as we knew it completely changed and some women friends still swear that there won't be a comeback especially for the bra, which makes me laugh.

By the beginning of May 2020, the pandemic was global. People had sadly lost their loved ones, with many passing away without warning at home, or in hospitals and nursing homes without their family or proper goodbyes, leaving behind broken hearts and people whose lives will never be the same again. A worrying outcome of this pandemic in the United Kingdom was the incessant debate about BAME (black and ethnic minority) people being more likely to die than their Caucasian counterparts. Experts and individuals gave reasons ranging from racism, lack of opportunity, inequality, poverty to education, however I beg to differ from that line of reasoning. In my humble opinion, I feel like most of our Caucasian counterparts, BAME people especially after the age of forty must adopt some life changing habits. We need to seek healthcare more to help in finding present underlying conditions or preventing the occurrence of one in future, we should develop healthier eating habits, and exercise culture for better health outcomes such as heart health, and take regular breaks and holidays, for cellular rejuvenation and rest. Combining all these will effectively make us healthier, and give us a fighting chance to beat unexpected diseases or viruses like COVID-19.

The virus is still here as I write albeit lockdown is now being eased in stages, with the country almost completely open with safety restrictions in place. Death rates are down, kids are going back to regular schooling in September, David is still working from home, we actually moved homes during this period, we have finally met family members and I have attended two small BBQs in the garden. Most people are choosing so staycations, we have no overseas holiday booked until October and December 2020, and we are hoping a vaccine is out by then. We are holding our breath for another wave of the coronavirus SARS2 virus, I have taken steps to lose weight and keep healthy with family, and I am completing my book. This year has been a roller coaster of emotions with the fear of having an unknown and unexpected virus, the possibility of sickness and death but thank God, we are all together and well. In all these, I have learnt life and family is all that matters, and that love and companionship is the most basic need of man. I pray this virus goes away and that we find an answer soon, in the mean time live healthy, stay alert, and keep safe.

MUSINGS EPISODE 8: MONEY MATTERS

"Money does not grow on trees"(**Anonymous**)

You see, I love money and arguably believe in the goodness of its' possession, so much so that I occasionally play the lottery even though I am yet to match 3-5 numbers on my numerous lucky dips. For some reason I am unaware of, I am too scared to choose my own numbers, maybe I want some supernatural arrangement to match things for me? I do not know honestly. I dabble into business, I am writing this now, whilst planning to launch an exclusive matrimony website, all in the bid to enter into the realm of wealth and riches. I continue to strive to attain financial comfort and freedom ever since I realized the impossibility of me transferring my nursing career to my children, but understanding that they can easily inherit a company or business in my name, giving them a head start to financial freedom. Money is vital to existence, and we hear a lot of about spending, saving and investing it. Now more than ever, the economic status veers more towards investing than saving, with record low interest rates and a high demand for spending. The pound is arguably one of the strongest currencies n the world and the United Kingdom is fertile ground for business and investment purposes. I have tried my hardest to work diligently to earn money when not pregnant and having my 3 babies, as I have morning or should I say all day sickness for the first fifteen weeks of pregnancy, which makes me utterly miserable and unable to do anything worthwhile.

I have in the past achieved a good regular income selling Bollywood movies, skincare products, branded cosmetics and perfumes on EBay and Amazon up until 2017, when I started my university degree and struggled to meet up with customer demands, resulting in my shops getting closed through poor time management. However, I work part time now and I strongly feel business is the way for me and I will surely find my way back at some point, God helping me. In 2013, the hubby and I accidently got into the buy to let market whilst looking for a new residential property and considering buying an upscale car and it has been my best financial decision in 10 years, we have refinanced and used the cash for consolidating debt, paying school fees, buying other small investments and supporting income. It is imperative to have solid plans for retirement and in my humble opinion, the best option is the tried and very trusted brick and mortal solution, meaning short to long-term property investment. My goal is to build a property portfolio slowly, using sourcing connections and on the market listings, managing properties through high street estate agents for peace of mind, as they will perform due diligence for occupants, streamline candidates and help prevent the horror rental stories.

In addition, I am also conducting personal research on short lets such as Airing, the Buy, Refurbish, and Refinance (BRR) model for deposit recycling, and car parks in city centers or airports. I do save a little by buying the United kingdom National Savings and Investments (NS&I) premium bonds, a government backed, tax free savings account which although pays no interest, puts your money put in an automatic lottery every month with the chance of winning from a million pounds to twenty-five pounds. Premium bonds are safe, your money is secure forever, you can withdraw within three working days to nominated bank account, winnings are paid by cheque and can be reinvested, and I might just win a million pounds this year!

Food for thought: I have learnt that how far you reach in investing depends on hard work, careful planning, an astute investment mind and mentoring from someone who has done what you intend to achieve. There are diverse investment products and techniques, and it is vital to perform due diligence, extensive research, and choose what works well for you as an individual, as there is no one size fits all, and no quick money making scheme ever works. Realistically, albeit for a few high-income earners, a steady job with the promise of a pension at the end will not suffice to maintain our current lifestyles in retirement, and a simple way of determining this is to try if you can maintain your current lifestyle without any income for the next six months, if your answer is yes you are good to go, if the answer is no then like me you need an option B, to achieve a comfortable retirement life.

MUSINGS EPISODE 9: I AM A CHRISTIAN SO WHAT?

"There is no other name under heaven, by which men are saved except Jesus" **Acts 4: 12.**

This chapter is quite interesting for me to muse about. You might question why this chapter, and why I am including this topic in my musings. My answer is that every individual has three aspects: the spiritual, the physical, and the intellectual. Hence, the importance of introducing my spiritual aspect to you in detail, alongside my other aspects. I respect everyone's opinions, values, beliefs, and spiritual preference, but I am unapologetically Christ like. I believe in the trinity of Jehovah, Jesus Christ, and the Holy Spirit, and I accept the bible as an absolute no questions asked, which is not me being gullible, but me attaining a good understanding of whom I serve. I was born into an orthodox Christian family, I am Anglican by birth however I gave my life to Jesus Christ at the age of 16 years after a life threatening accident which resulted in my not walking for 7 months, I must say I prayed myself up, and got healed of osteomyelitis an inflammation of the bone marrow in my left foot and my life completely changed.

So, what does being a Christian entail, especially in a country like the United Kingdom where people are religion weary, uninterested, or dare I say vague about life outside of the physical, attributing life to science, with some people regard the bible as false teachings, missing truths, and God is deemed wicked, violent, intolerant, or non inclusive? To avoid being stereotyped, Christians often have to sadly compromise and hide some of their beliefs and values in the bid to become socially accepted or compliant, but this is my take on the matter: if you have the right to disbelief and expect acceptance however you choose to live, then I have the right to believe and to expect acceptance, with no one questioning the other, for that in itself is tolerance. Someone once said the church is not a community club where anything goes, but I believe it should be a place where everyone is welcome to change, just not a place without rules or boundaries in the name of inclusiveness, because the bible is true and complete, and nothing in it can be changed, limited or adapted to fit in with our perceptions or opinions. Don't get me wrong I love everyone with the love of Christ hence I have friends, and even family with different beliefs, religion, values, outlook and orientation, however I am unapologetically, passionate about the sanctity of the bible and the words of God.

Practicing Christianity at home and in church is very easy for me, but the outside world is starkly different as it is not widely acceptable to share your religious beliefs, or faith with others. For example as a nurse, I am not allowed to share my faith or try to convert anyone at work, as it is deemed as violating their human right or personal space. I enjoy being a Christian, the lifestyle choices, church, the atmosphere, the activities, company of other Christians and was not surprised to read a 2020 news reporting that a Harvard research team found men and women who attended religious services weekly had a 33 per cent and 68 per cent lower risk of death from despair, and fatal illnesses as a result of alcohol and drugs, compared to those never attended. They stated that spiritual church activities provide a sense of hope and meaning in the face of panic, grief, suicidal thoughts, and teachings helps us see the human body as a 'temple' worthy of protection and care, which could limit consumption of harmful substances. Honestly, I have on many occasions pondered on how I would have survived the numerous health, marriage, family, kids, and financial challenges without my faith, and decided it would have been near impossible. I find peace, joy, safety, and security and in the power of Jesus Christ, that I can do all things through Christ who strengthens me, comfort in the knowledge that when I am weak, God is strong, for in HIM all things are possible, and my tomorrow will be all right. Hallelujah.

MUSINGS EPISODE 10: MY LIFE MY WORLD

"Do not be afraid of moving slowly, be afraid only of not moving at all" **Chinese proverb**

I am a woman… I am a black woman… I am a black woman living in a white world: looking for respect, inclusiveness, equality, and true freedom. I have a desire to impact, influence, create, and make a difference in my world whilst remaining true to myself. This is the last chapter of my memoir, the first lot of my musings. I hope you laughed, asked questions, agreed, disagreed, and maybe cried whilst reading my thoughts and experiences. Memories are part of our identity, so no matter who you are and no matter where in the world you find yourself: take that bold step, do something, make a change, live your life to the best of your ability, stay true to yourself and respect others, but never compromise or lower your belief or values for acceptance, nor let anyone make you feel inferior. Be proud of your identity, love yourself because you are beautiful, enjoy being different, develop healthy habits, get that health check, if you are struggling seek help, maybe find a faith it does help, be kind to others, appreciate love, family and friends, nurture your relationships. Stay happy no matter what, do what makes you happy. Develop and nurture your relationships. Work hard. Relax. Take holidays. Invest and save. Stay happy. Eat good food. Have faith. Believe in something or you fall for anything. Keep safe. Be tolerant.

Remember, *"Life is a journey, a journey you alone are responsible for the quality and experience, and even as you consider others, you must live first for yourself"* Helen Akangbe.